© **Copyright 2021 - All rights reserved.**

You may not reproduce, duplicate or send the contents of this book without direct written permission from the author. You cannot hereby despite any circumstance blame the publisher or hold him or her to legal responsibility for any reparation, compensations, or monetary forfeiture owing to the information included herein, either in a direct or an indirect way.

"Happiness is a butterfly, which when pursued, is always just beyond your grasp, but which, if you will sit down quietly, may alight upon you."

Nathaniel Hawthorne

Let your light shine

This Positivity Journal Belongs to :
_____
_____

YOU'VE TOTALLY GOT THIS!

"I've missed more than 9000 shots in my career. I've lost almost 300 games. 26 times I've been trusted to take the game winning shot and missed. I've failed over and over and over again in my life. And that is why I succeed."

Michael Jordan

DO Amazing THINGS!

Date   **Time**

Quoto of the day

Today I am truy grateful for

I am

Some amaizing things that happened today

What could I have done to make today even better?

Important Notes of the Day

Date _____ **Time** _____

Quoto of the day
_____
_____

Today I am truy grateful for
_____
_____
_____

I am
_____
_____
_____

Some amaizing things that happened today
_____
_____
_____
_____
_____
_____

What could I have done to make today even better?
_____
_____
_____

Important Notes of the Day

| Date | | Time | |

Quoto of the day

_____
_____
_____

Today I am truy grateful for

_____
_____
_____
_____

I am

_____
_____
_____
_____

Some amaizing things that happened today

_____
_____
_____
_____
_____
_____
_____

What could I have done to make today even better?

_____
_____
_____

Important Notes of the Day

Date _____ **Time** _____

Quoto of the day
_____
_____

Today I am truy grateful for
_____
_____
_____

I am
_____
_____
_____

Some amaizing things that happened today
_____
_____
_____
_____
_____

What could I have done to make today even better?
_____
_____

Important Notes of the Day

Date _____ **Time** _____

Quoto of the day
_____
_____
_____

Today I am truy grateful for
_____
_____
_____
_____

I am
_____
_____
_____

Some amaizing things that happened today
_____
_____
_____
_____
_____
_____
_____

What could I have done to make today even better?
_____
_____
_____

Important Notes of the Day

| Date | | Time | |

Quoto of the day

_____
_____
_____

Today I am truy grateful for

_____
_____
_____
_____

I am

_____
_____
_____
_____

Some amaizing things that happened today

_____
_____
_____
_____
_____
_____
_____

What could I have done to make today even better?

_____
_____
_____

Important Notes of the Day

Date _____ **Time** _____

Quoto of the day
_____
_____
_____

Today I am truy grateful for
_____
_____
_____
_____

I am
_____
_____
_____
_____

Some amaizing things that happened today
_____
_____
_____
_____
_____
_____
_____

What could I have done to make today even better?
_____
_____

Important Notes of the Day

Date _____ **Time** _____

Quoto of the day
_____
_____

Today I am truy grateful for
_____
_____
_____

I am
_____
_____
_____

Some amaizing things that happened today
_____
_____
_____
_____
_____

What could I have done to make today even better?
_____
_____

Important Notes of the Day

| Date | | Time | |

Quoto of the day

Today I am truy grateful for

I am

Some amaizing things that happened today

What could I have done to make today even better?

Important Notes of the Day

Date _____ **Time** _____

Quoto of the day
_____
_____

Today I am truy grateful for
_____
_____
_____

I am
_____
_____
_____

Some amaizing things that happened today
_____
_____
_____
_____
_____
_____

What could I have done to make today even better?
_____
_____

Important Notes of the Day

| Date | | Time | |

Quoto of the day

Today I am truy grateful for

I am

Some amaizing things that happened today

What could I have done to make today even better?

Important Notes of the Day

Date		Time	

Quoto of the day

_____
_____
_____

Today I am truy grateful for

_____
_____
_____
_____

I am

_____
_____
_____
_____

Some amaizing things that happened today

_____
_____
_____
_____
_____
_____
_____

What could I have done to make today even better?

_____
_____

Important Notes of the Day

Date **Time**

Quoto of the day

Today I am truy grateful for

I am

Some amaizing things that happened today

What could I have done to make today even better?

Important Notes of the Day

Date _____ **Time** _____

Quoto of the day
_____
_____

Today I am truy grateful for
_____
_____
_____

I am
_____
_____
_____

Some amaizing things that happened today
_____
_____
_____
_____
_____

What could I have done to make today even better?
_____
_____
_____

Important Notes of the Day

| Date | | Time | |

Quoto of the day

_____
_____
_____

Today I am truy grateful for

_____
_____
_____
_____

I am

_____
_____
_____
_____

Some amaizing things that happened today

_____
_____
_____
_____
_____
_____
_____

What could I have done to make today even better?

_____
_____

Important Notes of the Day

Date _____ **Time** _____

Quoto of the day
_____
_____

Today I am truy grateful for
_____
_____
_____

I am
_____
_____
_____

Some amaizing things that happened today
_____
_____
_____
_____
_____
_____

What could I have done to make today even better?
_____
_____

Important Notes of the Day

Date		Time	

Quoto of the day

Today I am truy grateful for

I am

Some amaizing things that happened today

What could I have done to make today even better?

Important Notes of the Day

| Date | | Time | |

Quoto of the day

Today I am truy grateful for

I am

Some amaizing things that happened today

What could I have done to make today even better?

Important Notes of the Day

| Date | | Time | |

Quoto of the day

Today I am truy grateful for

I am

Some amaizing things that happened today

What could I have done to make today even better?

Important Notes of the Day

Date		Time	

Quoto of the day

Today I am truy grateful for

I am

Some amaizing things that happened today

What could I have done to make today even better?

Important Notes of the Day

| Date | | Time | |

Quoto of the day

Today I am truy grateful for

I am

Some amaizing things that happened today

What could I have done to make today even better?

Important Notes of the Day

Date _____ **Time** _____

Quoto of the day
_____
_____
_____

Today I am truy grateful for
_____
_____
_____
_____

I am
_____
_____
_____
_____

Some amaizing things that happened today
_____
_____
_____
_____
_____
_____
_____

What could I have done to make today even better?
_____
_____

Important Notes of the Day

Date		Time	

Quoto of the day

Today I am truy grateful for

I am

Some amaizing things that happened today

What could I have done to make today even better?

Important Notes of the Day

Date		Time	

Quoto of the day

_____
_____
_____

Today I am truy grateful for

_____
_____
_____
_____

I am

_____
_____
_____
_____

Some amaizing things that happened today

_____
_____
_____
_____
_____
_____
_____

What could I have done to make today even better?

_____
_____

Important Notes of the Day

Date		Time	

Quoto of the day

Today I am truy grateful for

I am

Some amaizing things that happened today

What could I have done to make today even better?

Important Notes of the Day

Date		Time	

Quoto of the day

Today I am truy grateful for

I am

Some amaizing things that happened today

What could I have done to make today even better?

Important Notes of the Day

Date: _____ Time: _____

Quoto of the day
_____
_____
_____

Today I am truy grateful for
_____
_____
_____
_____

I am
_____
_____
_____
_____

Some amaizing things that happened today
_____
_____
_____
_____
_____
_____
_____

What could I have done to make today even better?
_____
_____

Important Notes of the Day

Date   **Time**

Quoto of the day

_____
_____

Today I am truy grateful for

_____
_____
_____

I am

_____
_____
_____

Some amaizing things that happened today

_____
_____
_____
_____
_____
_____
_____

What could I have done to make today even better?

_____
_____

Important Notes of the Day

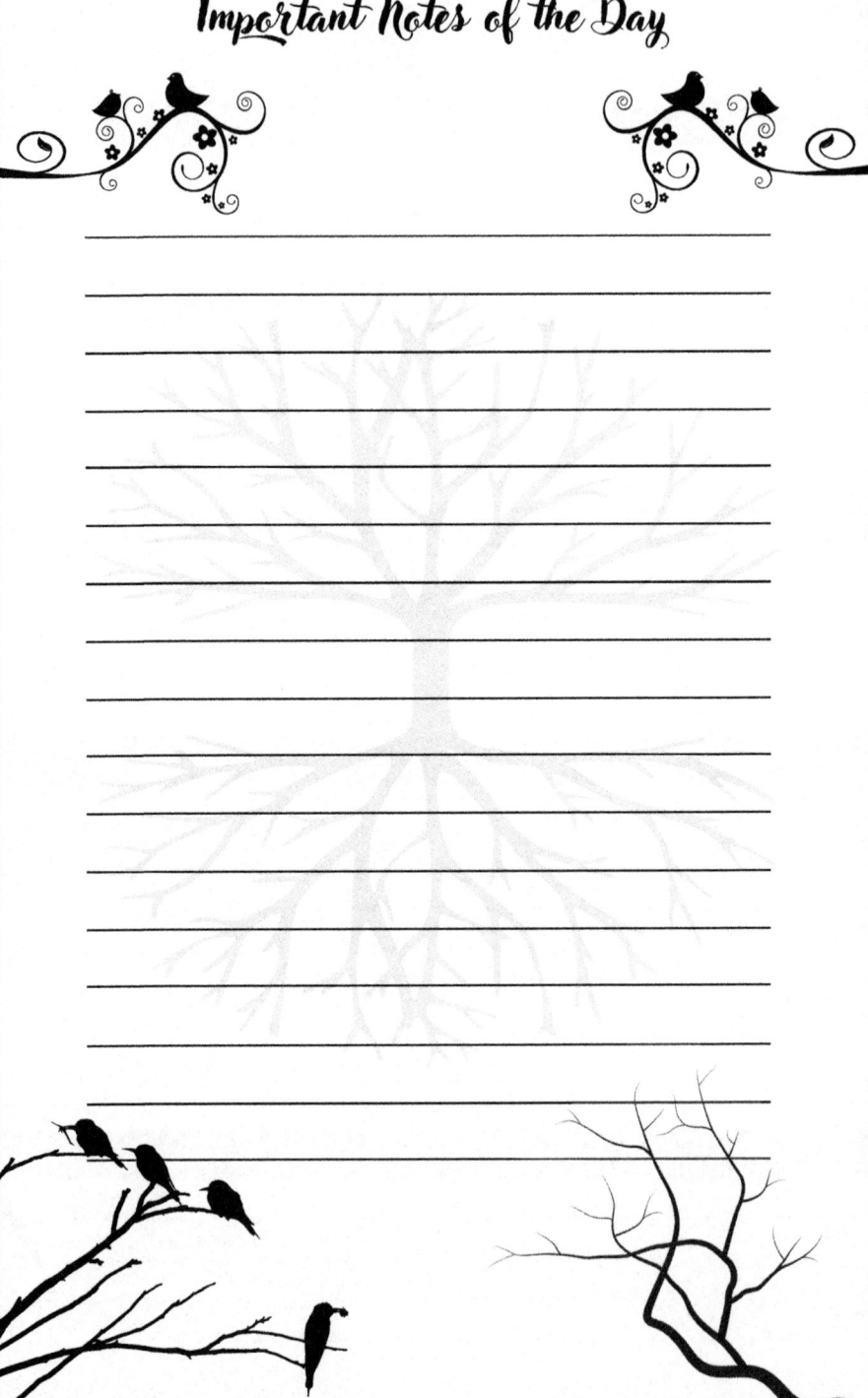

Date _____ **Time** _____

Quoto of the day

_____
_____

Today I am truy grateful for

_____
_____
_____

I am

_____
_____
_____

Some amaizing things that happened today

_____
_____
_____
_____
_____
_____

What could I have done to make today even better?

_____
_____
_____

Important Notes of the Day

| Date | | Time | |

Quoto of the day

_____
_____
_____

Today I am truy grateful for

_____
_____
_____

I am

_____
_____
_____

Some amaizing things that happened today

_____
_____
_____
_____
_____
_____

What could I have done to make today even better?

_____
_____

Important Notes of the Day

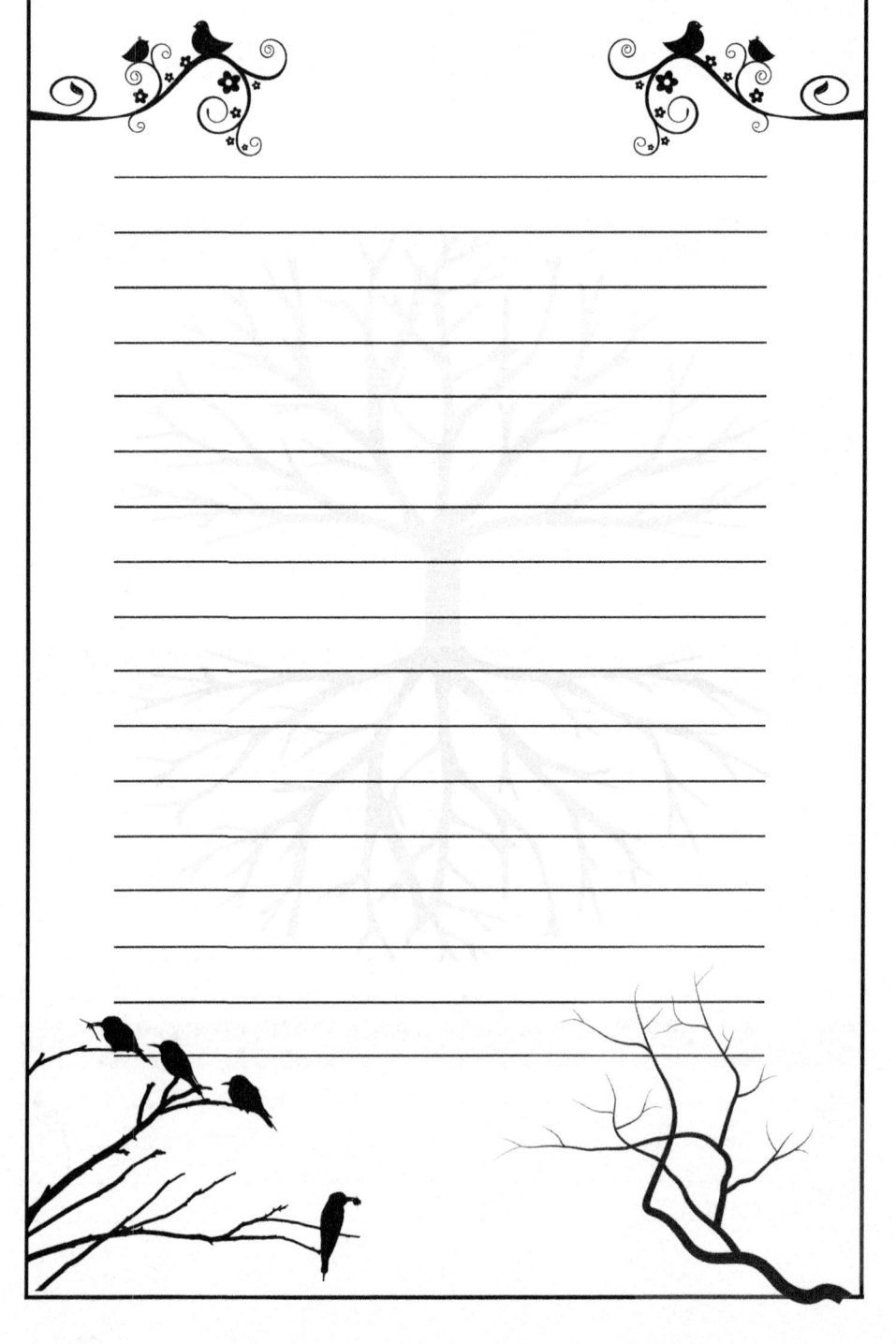

Date   Time

Quoto of the day

Today I am truy grateful for

I am

Some amaizing things that happened today

What could I have done to make today even better?

Important Notes of the Day

Date _____ **Time** _____

Quoto of the day
_____
_____

Today I am truy grateful for
_____
_____
_____

I am
_____
_____
_____

Some amaizing things that happened today
_____
_____
_____
_____
_____
_____

What could I have done to make today even better?
_____
_____

Important Notes of the Day

Date		Time	

Quoto of the day

_____
_____

Today I am truy grateful for

_____
_____
_____

I am

_____
_____
_____

Some amaizing things that happened today

_____
_____
_____
_____
_____
_____
_____

What could I have done to make today even better?

_____
_____

Important Notes of the Day

Date	Time

Quoto of the day

Today I am truy grateful for

I am

Some amaizing things that happened today

What could I have done to make today even better?

Important Notes of the Day

Date		Time	

Quoto of the day

Today I am truy grateful for

I am

Some amaizing things that happened today

What could I have done to make today even better?

Important Notes of the Day

| Date | | Time | |

Quoto of the day

_____
_____

Today I am truy grateful for

_____
_____
_____

I am

_____
_____
_____

Some amaizing things that happened today

_____
_____
_____
_____
_____
_____

What could I have done to make today even better?

_____
_____

Important Notes of the Day

Date _____ **Time** _____

Quoto of the day
_____
_____

Today I am truy grateful for
_____
_____
_____

I am
_____
_____
_____

Some amaizing things that happened today
_____
_____
_____
_____
_____
_____
_____

What could I have done to make today even better?
_____
_____

Important Notes of the Day

Date		Time	

Quoto of the day

Today I am truy grateful for

I am

Some amaizing things that happened today

What could I have done to make today even better?

Important Notes of the Day

| Date | | Time | |

Quoto of the day

Today I am truy grateful for

I am

Some amaizing things that happened today

What could I have done to make today even better?

Important Notes of the Day

| Date | | Time | |

Quoto of the day

_____
_____

Today I am truy grateful for

_____
_____
_____
_____

I am

_____
_____
_____
_____

Some amaizing things that happened today

_____
_____
_____
_____
_____
_____
_____

What could I have done to make today even better?

_____
_____

Important Notes of the Day

Date _____ **Time** _____

Quoto of the day
_____
_____
_____

Today I am truy grateful for
_____
_____
_____
_____

I am
_____
_____
_____
_____

Some amaizing things that happened today
_____
_____
_____
_____
_____
_____
_____

What could I have done to make today even better?
_____
_____
_____

Important Notes of the Day

| Date | | Time | |

Quoto of the day

_____
_____
_____

Today I am truy grateful for

_____
_____
_____
_____

I am

_____
_____
_____
_____

Some amaizing things that happened today

_____
_____
_____
_____
_____
_____
_____

What could I have done to make today even better?

_____
_____

Important Notes of the Day

Date _____ **Time** _____

Quoto of the day
_____
_____

Today I am truy grateful for
_____
_____
_____

I am
_____
_____
_____

Some amaizing things that happened today
_____
_____
_____
_____
_____
_____

What could I have done to make today even better?
_____
_____

Important Notes of the Day

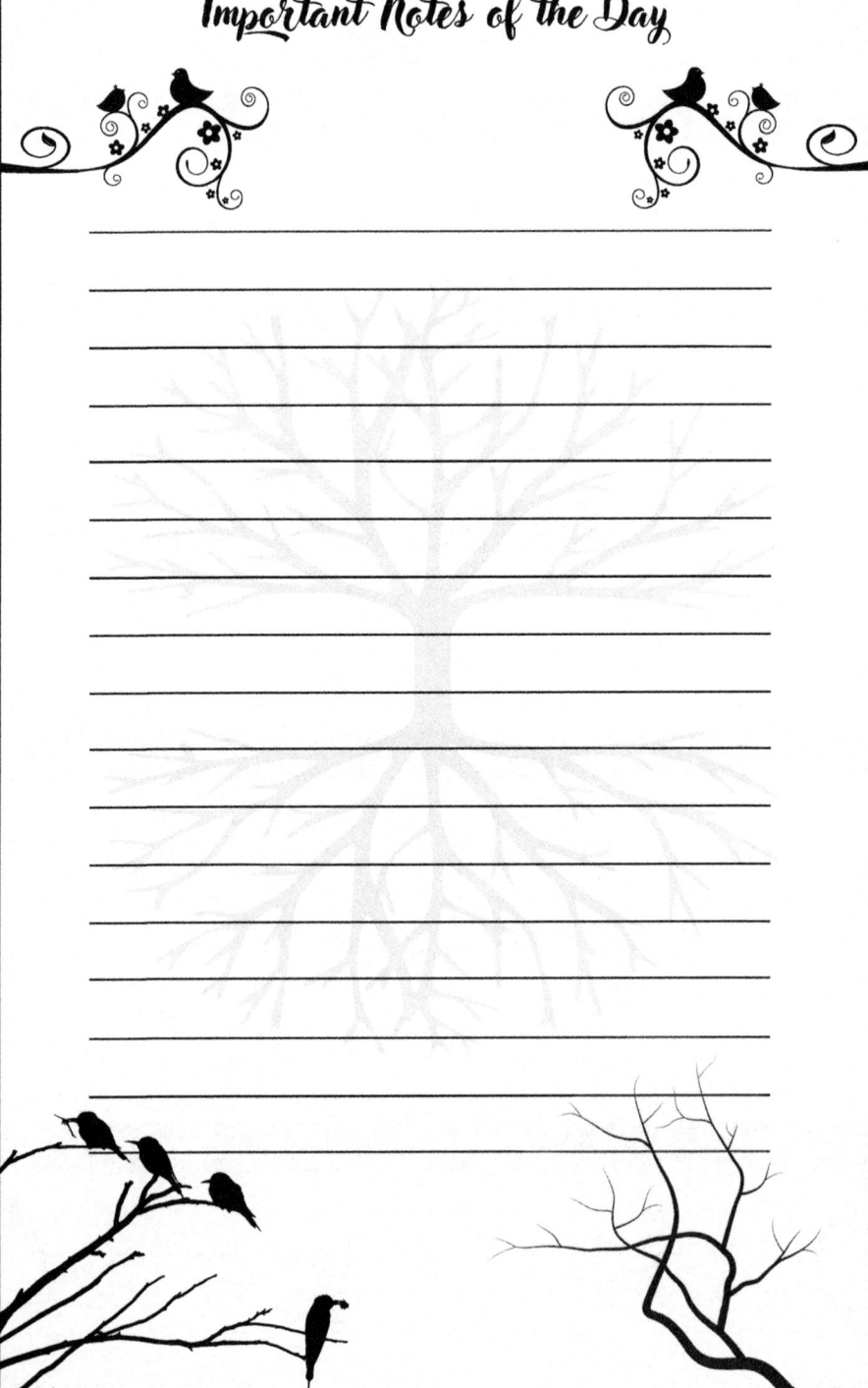

Date **Time**

Quoto of the day

___

Today I am truy grateful for

___

I am

___

Some amaizing things that happened today

___

What could I have done to make today even better?

Important Notes of the Day

| Date | | Time | |

Quoto of the day

Today I am truy grateful for

I am

Some amaizing things that happened today

What could I have done to make today even better?

Important Notes of the Day

| Date | | Time | |

Quoto of the day

Today I am truy grateful for

I am

Some amaizing things that happened today

What could I have done to make today even better?

Important Notes of the Day

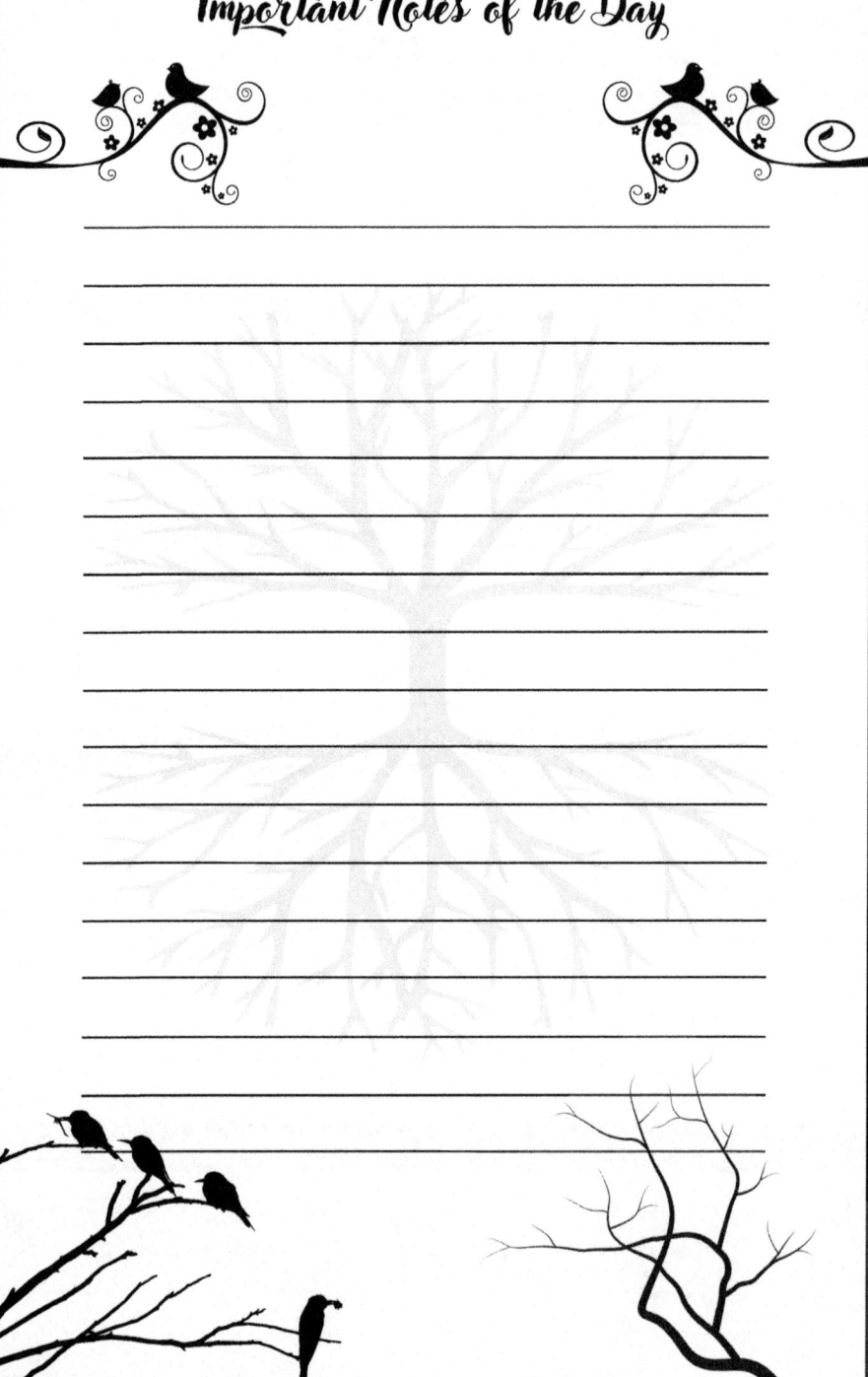

Date		Time	

Quoto of the day

Today I am truy grateful for

I am

Some amaizing things that happened today

What could I have done to make today even better?

Important Notes of the Day

| Date | | Time | |

Quoto of the day

Today I am truy grateful for

I am

Some amaizing things that happened today

What could I have done to make today even better?

Important Notes of the Day

| Date | | Time | |

Quoto of the day

___

Today I am truy grateful for

___

I am

___

Some amaizing things that happened today

___

What could I have done to make today even better?

Important Notes of the Day

Date: _____ Time: _____

Quoto of the day

_____
_____

Today I am truy grateful for

_____
_____
_____

I am

_____
_____
_____

Some amaizing things that happened today

_____
_____
_____
_____
_____
_____

What could I have done to make today even better?

_____
_____

Important Notes of the Day

We create our Books with lots of love and care.

But mistakes can always happen, so if there are any issues with your book such as faulty bindings or printing errors please contact the platform you bought it to get a replacement.

FOR QUESTIONS & SUGGESTIONS

Emails us at : lazy.black.cat.books@gmail.com

Thank you ! ♥